Food Dudes

BEN & JERRY:
Ice Cream Manufacturers

Joanne Mattern
ABDO Publishing Company

visit us at
www.abdopublishing.com

Published by ABDO Publishing Company, 8000 West 78th Street, Edina, Minnesota 55439.
Copyright © 2011 by Abdo Consulting Group, Inc. International copyrights reserved in all
countries. No part of this book may be reproduced in any form without written permission from the
publisher. The Checkerboard Library™ is a trademark and logo of ABDO Publishing Company.

Printed in the United States of America, North Mankato, Minnesota.
092010
012011

 PRINTED ON RECYCLED PAPER

Cover Photos: Getty Images
Interior Photos: Alamy pp. 15, 20; AP Images pp. 7, 8, 11, 16, 19, 21, 25;
    courtesy Ben & Jerry's Homemade Inc. p. 13; Corbis pp. 9, 22; Getty Images pp. 1, 5, 26;
    Photolibrary p. 24

Series Coordinator: BreAnn Rumsch
Editors: Tamara L. Britton, BreAnn Rumsch
Art Direction & Cover Design: Neil Klinepier

Library of Congress Cataloging-in-Publication Data

Mattern, Joanne, 1963-
  Ben & Jerry : ice cream manufacturers / Joanne Mattern.
    p. cm. -- (Food dudes)
  ISBN 978-1-61613-554-6
  1. Cohen, Ben (Ben R.)--Juvenile literature. 2. Greenfield, Jerry--Juvenile literature. 3. Ben &
Jerry's (Firm)--Juvenile literature. 4. Ice cream industry--United States--History--Juvenile literature.
5. Businessmen--United States--Biography--Juvenile literature. I. Title. II. Title: Ben and Jerry.
  HD9281.U54B466 2011
  338.7'63740922--dc22
  [B]
                                  2010027890

Contents

Born in Brooklyn

Ben & Jerry's Homemade ice cream has been pleasing customers since 1978. It is one of the most famous products to come from Vermont. However, Ben and Jerry are not from Vermont. They are from New York. In fact, they were born just days apart in the same hospital! Ben and Jerry met as young boys long before they became successful business partners.

Bennett Cohen was born on March 18, 1951, in Brooklyn, New York. His parents were Irving and Frances Cohen. Ben had an older sister named Alice. His father worked as an **accountant**. Ben's mother stayed home to care for the children.

Jerry Greenfield also began his life in Brooklyn. He was born four days before Ben on March 14, 1951. Jerry's parents were Malcolm and Mildred Greenfield. Jerry had an older sister named Ronnie. He also had a younger brother named Geff. Jerry's father worked as a **stockbroker**. His mother took care of the household.

Both Ben and Jerry loved food from the time they were young boys. But, their eating habits soon made them overweight. As a result, Ben was teased at school. Jerry's classmates teased him about his weight, too.

Today, Ben & Jerry's scoop shops operate in more than 25 countries throughout North America, Europe, Asia, and Australia.

A New Friendship

When Ben was young, his family moved to the town of Merrick on Long Island in New York. Jerry also grew up in Merrick. The two boys lived just a few miles from each other.

Ben and Jerry went to different elementary schools. They finally met in 1963 at Merrick Avenue Junior High School. The boys were in the same seventh grade gym class. Yet because they were overweight, neither Ben nor Jerry was very **athletic**.

One day, the boys had to run around the school track. The teacher thought they ran too slowly. He threatened to make them run around the track a second time. But, Ben felt this was unfair. He argued that another run would not make them run faster.

Jerry liked Ben's way of thinking. The two boys began spending time together. Yet, officials soon thought the school was becoming too crowded. So the next year, Ben and other students attended Brookside Junior High School.

Ben and Jerry have stayed friends throughout all
their years in school and business together.

School Days

In 1966, Ben and Jerry both entered Calhoun High School on Long Island. There, their friendship grew. The boys spent a lot of time together. They liked driving around in cars and hanging out at the local pizza parlor.

Though they were best friends, Ben and Jerry were very different. Jerry was a great student. He studied hard and got good grades. Ben was also smart, but he did not like school. He was not interested in doing what the teachers told him. And, he did not want to study subjects he didn't like. Because of this, Ben's grades were not as good as Jerry's.

Both boys graduated from high school in 1969. Jerry graduated third in a class of more than 600 students. And, he was awarded a **National Merit Scholarship**. After high school, Jerry attended Oberlin College in Oberlin, Ohio. He thought he wanted to be a doctor. So, he took classes to prepare himself for medical school.

Ben was not interested in college. But, his parents wanted him to have a good education. Ben did not want to disappoint them, so he chose to attend Colgate University in Hamilton, New York.

Ben (left) and Jerry (right) used their differences to make their company stronger.

Drifting Around

Ben struggled at Colgate. He learned he did not like college any better than high school. He thought his classes were boring. So in 1970, Ben left college.

After that, Ben did many different things. He traveled to California. Then, he visited Jerry at Oberlin. Ben also worked at the Pied Piper ice cream company in New York.

After a while, Ben decided to give college another try. In 1971, he entered Skidmore College in Saratoga Springs, New York. There, Ben learned how to make **pottery** and jewelry.

To help pay for these classes, Ben held several jobs. He worked at Anne's Coffee Park Diner. Ben also mopped floors at a department store. And, he mopped floors at a restaurant called Friendly's. Ben liked his art classes. Still, he only stayed at Skidmore for one year.

In 1972, Ben moved to New York City, New York. There, he held many different jobs. He never liked working at any one place for too long. Ben worked the night shift at a hospital. He also delivered pottery wheels. He even drove a taxi!

Ben was a creative person. Later in life, he used his ideas to help turn Ben & Jerry's into a successful business.

Then in 1974, Ben got a new job. He was hired to teach crafts at Highland Community School in Paradox, New York. Highland was a school for troubled teenagers. There, Ben taught the students **pottery**, photography, and **silk-screening**. He also helped them write and create a short movie. Finally, Ben had found a job he enjoyed.

A Tasty Idea

Meanwhile, Jerry did well at Oberlin. He graduated in 1973. However, his grades were not good enough to qualify for medical school.

So, Jerry got a job in a laboratory in New York City. In 1974, he tried again to get into medical school. But once again, Jerry was not accepted.

Soon after, Jerry fell in love with a woman named Elizabeth Skarie. Elizabeth was a nursing student. After graduation, she was offered a job in North Carolina. Jerry decided to follow Elizabeth there. He got a job in North Carolina, too. But by 1977, their relationship ended.

That same year, the school where Ben worked closed. Ben and Jerry decided it was time to start in a new direction. They planned to open a business together. Jerry said, "Since we love to eat, we immediately thought of food." So, the two friends decided to open an ice cream parlor.

Ben and Jerry's love of ice cream made the choice for their business together obvious!

Off to Vermont

Cohen and Greenfield knew they had a lot to learn before opening their business. So, they visited many ice cream shops. They also learned how to make ice cream.

The two friends found a **correspondence course** through Pennsylvania State University. They split the five dollars it cost to take the class. Greenfield studied the science of ice cream and Cohen experimented with recipes. They even got help from a professor at the University of Vermont.

From experience, Cohen and Greenfield knew that college students love to eat ice cream. So, they decided to open their store near Skidmore College. At that time, there were no ice cream shops in Saratoga Springs. Cohen and Greenfield thought the lack of competition would help them succeed.

Then, Cohen and Greenfield faced a big problem. Someone else opened an ice cream shop in Saratoga Springs! Cohen and Greenfield decided they should open their business somewhere else. So, they searched for a different college town.

Cohen and Greenfield eventually settled on Burlington, Vermont. Burlington is a small city on the shores of Lake Champlain. The University of Vermont is located there.

Today, the main Burlington Ben & Jerry's scoop shop is located on Church Street.

Hard Work

The original scoop shop was open from 1978 to 1982.

Next, Cohen and Greenfield had to raise money. They needed it to buy equipment and run their business. Cohen and Greenfield borrowed $4,000 from the bank. Cohen's father also lent them some money. Ben & Jerry's Homemade Inc. was **incorporated** on December 17, 1977.

Soon after, Cohen and Greenfield found a place to start their ice cream shop. It was an old gas station, but they thought it was in a good location.

Even though the location was great, the building was in terrible shape. The roof leaked, and the ceiling was falling down. It was the middle of winter, so the floor was covered with ice.

Cohen and Greenfield worked hard to fix the building. They asked their friend Darrell Mullis to help them. Mullis agreed to do the work. His payment was free ice cream for life!

The two friends also worked hard to create great ice cream. Cohen had a very bad sense of taste. He could only taste foods with strong flavors. So, Greenfield created recipes with more flavor than any other ice cream available. Cohen also liked big chunks of chocolate, nuts, and fruit in his ice cream. Greenfield added those ingredients to their recipes.

Cohen and Greenfield's ice cream was delicious. They used the best ingredients they could find. But, premium ingredients were expensive. So, the friends barely had enough money left to feed themselves. Their diet consisted of ice cream, saltine crackers, and canned fish.

Scooping Success

The first Ben & Jerry's Homemade scoop shop opened for business on May 5, 1978. For the first day, they advertised "buy one, get one free." Small cones sold for 55¢. The store was crowded with people. They loved the rich-tasting ice cream that came in unusual flavors!

So many people came to buy ice cream that Cohen and Greenfield ran out after just a few days! To keep up with demand, they had to buy a new ice cream hardener. This allowed them to freeze larger quantities of ice cream faster.

At first, Cohen and Greenfield each worked about 100 hours a week! Still, they wanted their company to be fun. So, they organized exciting events in the community. One popular event was called Fall Down. There, Cohen and Greenfield held contests for ice cream eating, stilt walking, frog jumping, and more!

The two friends wanted their customers to enjoy coming to their scoop shop, too. So, they showed free movies on the wall of the building next door. On May 5, 1979, customers helped them celebrate their first year in business. That day, Cohen and Greenfield handed out free ice cream cones!

Many Ben & Jerry's scoop shops still celebrate Free Cone Day in honor of the company's anniversary.

Pint-Sized Plan

In just a few months, Cohen and Greenfield had created a very popular product. Soon, restaurants asked if they could stock Ben & Jerry's ice cream. In January 1979, Cohen and Greenfield began delivering large cartons of ice cream to restaurants. Cohen drove the cartons around Vermont and New York in a car. But, he couldn't keep this up for long.

The partners soon took out another loan for their company. This time, they were able to borrow $30,000. With it, they opened a factory. There, they could make enough ice cream to meet demand. They also bought a delivery truck.

Ben & Jerry's began offering factory tours in Waterbury, Vermont, in 1986. Today, these tours remain a popular attraction.

Next, Cohen and Greenfield decided to offer their ice cream to grocery stores. In 1980, they began selling eight flavors in pint-sized cartons. To keep up with demand, they opened another factory in 1981.

Soon, people all over the country wanted Ben & Jerry's ice cream! Other people even started their own Ben & Jerry's scoop shops. They paid Cohen and Greenfield to use the company's name and ice cream. In June 1981, the first Ben & Jerry's **franchise** opened in Shelburne, Vermont.

Selling pints turned out to be the secret to Cohen (above) *and Greenfield's success.*

Giving Back

Cohen and Greenfield liked running their business in a way that treated their employees well. They believed the highest-paid employee should not earn more than five times what the lowest-paid employee earned. So, all employees were fairly **compensated**.

Employees enjoyed numerous **benefits**, too. These included day care at work and good health plans. Employees also shared 5 percent of the

company's profits. And, they received three free pints of ice cream every day they worked!

Cohen and Greenfield also wanted to give back to the community. So, they thought of ways to give back through normal business activities. One idea was to help open special scoop shops that gave jobs to people in troubled neighborhoods.

Then in 1985, Cohen and Greenfield started the Ben & Jerry's Foundation. This organization supports community groups throughout the United States. Each year, Ben & Jerry's funds the foundation with 7.5 percent of the company's profits. This is a large amount! Most companies only give away about 1.5 percent of their profits.

In 1988, Cohen and Greenfield committed their business beliefs to a **mission statement**. It states that Ben & Jerry's will make the best ice cream possible. It also promises the company will continue helping the community.

Cohen and Greenfield were interested in ideas other than their own.
They encouraged employees to share their thoughts about the company.

Cohen and Greenfield continued using their ice cream to support issues they believed in. In 1988, Cohen founded a group called One Percent for Peace. This group's goal is to redirect 1 percent of the U.S. defense budget to peace-promoting projects.

That same year, Ben & Jerry's sold ice cream bars called Peace Pops. The packaging had a message about supporting One Percent for Peace.

Cohen and Greenfield also made efforts to save the **environment**. They gave money to support environmental groups.

Then in 1989, Cohen created a new ice cream flavor called Rainforest Crunch. It contained nuts that were grown on trees in the Amazon rain

Rainforest Crunch

Cohen and Greenfield believed in addressing social needs while still making money. This made their company much different from most successful businesses.

forest. Buying these nuts helped prevent the trees from being cut down. And, some of the profits went to help native nut growers.

In 1991, Cohen and Greenfield held their first annual One World One Heart Festival. This event did more than support a cause. It encouraged others to get involved in political issues. People could get free ice cream at the event by writing postcards to their **legislators**.

Later Life

Cohen and Greenfield are proud they used their business's success to help others live better lives.

Cohen and Greenfield enjoyed many years of success at their company. In 2000, a large food company called Unilever wanted to buy Ben & Jerry's. Cohen and Greenfield agreed to sell their business.

After the sale, Cohen and Greenfield continued to give their time and money to their communities. Greenfield remained with the company to manage the Ben & Jerry's Foundation.

Cohen moved on to other projects. He started a group called True Majority. True Majority works to pass laws that help children and the **environment**. It also encourages citizens to speak up about political issues.

In their free time, Cohen and Greenfield like to spend time with their families. Greenfield and Elizabeth had reunited and were married in 1987. In 1988, they had a son named Tyrone. Cohen was married for a time. He and his wife Cindy had a daughter named Aretha in 1990.

Ben Cohen and Jerry Greenfield did not follow the usual rules to start their business. Instead, they did things their own way. Today, their ice cream makes many people happy. But Ben & Jerry's Homemade is about more than good ice cream. It proved that a business can address social needs and be successful at the same time.

Timeline

1951	In Brooklyn, New York, Jerry Greenfield was born on March 14 and Bennett Cohen was born on March 18.
1969	Ben and Jerry graduated from Calhoun High School on Long Island in New York.
1973	Jerry graduated from Oberlin College in Oberlin, Ohio.
1978	On May 5, Cohen and Greenfield opened their first Ben & Jerry's Homemade ice cream scoop shop in Burlington, Vermont.
1980	Cohen and Greenfield began selling ice cream pints in grocery stores.
1981	The first Ben & Jerry's franchise opened in Shelburne, Vermont.
1985	Cohen and Greenfield started the Ben & Jerry's Foundation.
1988	Cohen founded One Percent for Peace; Cohen and Greenfield wrote the Ben & Jerry's mission statement.
1991	Cohen and Greenfield held their first annual One World One Heart Festival.
2000	Cohen and Greenfield sold Ben & Jerry's Homemade to Unilever.

The Flavor Scoop

Every year, Ben & Jerry's releases several new flavors. Some are sold in pints and others are sold at scoop shops. Over the years, several flavors have become huge, lasting hits with ice cream lovers. Other flavors have been retired and sent to the Ben & Jerry's Flavor Graveyard. Do you have a favorite flavor that is no longer sold? What great flavors do you think Ben & Jerry's will invent next?

HERE ARE SOME BEN & JERRY'S FLAVOR MILESTONES:

New York Super Fudge Chunk - 1985

Cherry Garcia - 1987

Chunky Monkey - 1988

Chocolate Fudge Brownie - 1990

Chocolate Chip Cookie Dough - 1991

Chubby Hubby - 1995

Phish Food - 1997

Neapolitan Dynamite - 2006

Americone Dream - 2007

Glossary

accountant - someone who records the amounts of money made and spent by a person or a business.

athletic - physically active and strong.

benefit - a service or a right provided by an employer in addition to wages or salary. Common benefits include health insurance and vacation time.

compensate - to make a payment to, especially for work done or to make up for a loss.

correspondence course - a form of schooling in which lessons and exercises are mailed to a student. When completed, the lessons are returned to a correspondence school for grading.

environment - all the surroundings that affect the growth and well-being of a living thing.

franchise - the right granted to someone to sell a company's goods or services in a particular place. The business operating with this right is also known as a franchise.

incorporate - to form into a legal corporation.

legislator - a person who makes laws.

mission statement - an objective or purpose established by a company. It guides the daily business and activities of workers and executives.

National Merit Scholarship - a gift of money high school students may compete to receive. Winners are chosen based on their abilities, skills, and accomplishments.

pottery - clayware. Pottery is also the art or craft of making clayware.

silk-screening - a printing method. A design is produced by forcing colored ink through a fabric screen. The screen is treated so that the ink can pass through some areas and not others.

stockbroker - a person that handles orders to buy and sell stocks. Stocks are the shares or portions into which a company or a business is divided.

Web Sites

To learn more about Ben & Jerry, visit ABDO Publishing Company online. Web sites about Ben & Jerry are featured on our Book Links page. These links are routinely monitored and updated to provide the most current information available.

www.abdopublishing.com

Index